BRAVE SCOTS

WILLIAM WALLACE

WRITTEN BY

GARY SMAILES

ILLUSTRATED BY

CRAIG HOWARTH

For my wife, Caroline
G. Smailes

First published in paperback in Great Britain 2006

Design - Winsome Malcolm

Reprographics - GWP Graphics

Printing - Printer Trento, Italy

Published by

GW Publishing
PO Box 6091
Thatcham
Berks
RG19 8XZ

Tel +44 (0) 1635 268080

www.gwpublishing.com

ISBN 09551564-5-9
978-09551564-5-8

William Wallace was a Brave Scot and a hero. It is no surprise that hundreds of books have been written about his great deeds. Unfortunately many of these have been based on myth and ignored the real man behind the legend. This book tells the true story of William Wallace, and since you are all sensible and intelligent readers, the bits that no one ever wanted you to know have been left in.

So if you are ready to discover the real story of William Wallace read on...

In medieval times England and Scotland were separate countries with their own laws, their own armies and most importantly, their own kings. The king of Scotland was a man called Alexander III. He was a good king, who united Scotland and even defeated an invading Viking army at the Battle of Largs in 1263.

Today the people of Scotland and England are friends … well almost … but this was not always the case. King Alexander III had made Scotland into a powerful country and not even Edward I, the mighty English king, dared to attack Scotland whilst Alexander was king.

On a stormy night in 1286 everything changed …

Alexander had spent the day at Edinburgh Castle and, despite a huge storm, decided to ride home. His journey took him along a dangerous cliff-top path and, about a mile from his house, disaster struck! The king's horse was panicked by a flash of lightning and stumbled too close to the cliff edge. He was thrown off the horse and plummeted to his death on the beach below.

This is all really sad, especially for Alexander, but he really should have known better. When he was younger a fortune teller had warned him that his horse would be the death of him. Thinking he could outwit the prophet, Alexander had immediately ordered his own horse to be killed. Unfortunately for the king (and his poor horse!), it turned out the fortune teller was right—it was just that the Scottish king had killed the wrong horse!

In medieval times it was thought that, if possible, only one family should rule a country. This meant that when a king died, his son or daughter would become the next king or queen. This was all fine if he had lots of happy children running around waiting to be crowned, but this was not always the case. Medieval times were pretty dangerous and kids had a horrible habit of dropping dead from disease. This meant that if the dead king had no children, then it was the job of someone else in the king's family to fill the throne.

King John

With the king dead, the only member of Alexander's family left alive who could rule Scotland was his granddaughter, Margaret. However, it wasn't that straightforward — things never are! Margaret was not the perfect choice for a Scottish queen, since not only did she live in Norway, but she was only five years old! Unfortunately crafty King Edward had a plan and he arranged for Margaret to sail to Scotland and marry his five-year-old son. At first everything was going fine, but on the voyage young Margaret became ill and soon died.

This left Scotland without a king and with the throne empty, lots of people started to think that they would be the perfect choice for the next king of Scotland. In fact, it seemed that almost anyone with the slightest link to a dead Scottish king thought they would make a good monarch.

Despite lots of talking and arguing, the Scottish people couldn't decide who should be the next king. So they asked Edward, king of England, who he thought should be crowned—big mistake! The Scots had forgotten one of the golden rules of living in the medieval Britain — never trust an English king! Crafty King

Edward selected a man called John Balliol. Edward chose Balliol, not because he thought that he would make the best King and help Scotland to be strong and powerful …no, Edward chose Balliol because he was weak and would do exactly as Edward wanted. So in 1292, to the horror of the Scots people, John Balliol became King John of Scotland.

The new king had a very tough job ahead of him. Not only did he have to stop the king of England invading Scotland, but he also had to make sure that the ancient Scottish clans didn't start fighting amongst themselves—poor King John.

NOW ROBERT, I HOPE WE CAN ALL BE FRIENDS AND HAVE NO MORE FIGHTING.

Crafty King Edward

England was ruled by King Edward I, who was a tough and unpopular king. He was given the nickname of 'Long Shanks', which meant long legs, but he deserved much worse. Edward was a very arrogant king who felt that he always knew what was best for his people. In fact, he felt that the whole of Britain would be better off if it was under his rule! So in 1282, when the Welsh prince Llywelyn ap Gruffudd rebelled, Edward knew exactly what was best for the Welsh people — he invaded them! The king's army bullied and beat the poor Welsh into submission and soon crushed all resistance.

Edward liked to control his subjects and one of his favourite hobbies was to pass new laws. However, these laws needed punishments and here are just a few of the worst:

HOW IS HE GOING TO SMELL?

PRETTY AWFUL!

Mutilation

The courts needed a way of showing that someone had been caught lying or cheating. To do this they would mutilate the criminal, cutting off bits of his body. In fact, no body part was safe, with an ear, a finger, a hand, a nose or even an eye often being removed.

Stocks

In the stocks criminals would be trapped by their arms and neck, making escape impossible. Large crowds would often gather around and start to throw things. If the crowd got bored, they would attack the criminal, sometimes even nailing his ears to the wooden stocks or, if they were feeling really horrible, cutting them off and running away with them!

Hanging

If the crime was really bad a criminal would be killed. The most common method of execution was hanging. However, this could sometimes take hours or even days. If the criminal was lucky, his friends would grab hold of his legs and swing, hoping to kill him quickly — with friends like those who needs enemies! If the king was feeling mean then he would ask for him to be hanged, drawn and quartered. The criminal would have his intestines cut out whilst he was still alive and burned in front of his eyes. Only then would he be hanged and the dead body cut into four sections, with each section being sent to a different location to serve as a warning for others.

Scotland Invaded!

Now you know a bit about King Edward you can see why it was such a mistake to get him involved in the choice of the Scottish king. Edward had always planned to rule Scotland, just like he did Wales; he was just waiting for the right moment. Luckily for the Scottish people, King John was not a pushover and he refused to be bullied by Edward. Instead he did what he thought was best for Scotland and even signed a treaty with France, which said they would help in any battle against the English. This just made the English king angry and he decided that if King John wouldn't do as he wanted, then he would take Scotland by force, just as he had done in Wales.

He ordered his army to march north and attack the town of Berwick. It was poorly defended and the army easily took control.

Unfortunately, the English soldiers were as arrogant as their king and wanted to teach the Scots a lesson. Once they had taken over Berwick they simply didn't stop killing for three days!

The Scots were angry and they quickly formed an army, which marched to meet the English on 27th April 1296 at Dunbar. The day went badly and the inexperienced Scottish warriors were easily defeated. It was a dark time for Scotland and it seemed that the country would soon be part of Edward's kingdom. The king's army marched through Scotland and eventually King John surrendered to Edward.

In a ceremony of defeat, King John was made to stand before the English monarch and his royal insignia was ripped from his shirt. From that day Balliol was known as Toom Tabard (empty coat).

However, all was not lost since one man did have the courage to stand up to Edward. His name was William Wallace and it was a name which the king would come to hate!

The Truth about William Wallace

HOW LONG DID THE BUILDERS SAY IT WOULD TAKE TO FINISH THE HOUSE?

OH, ABOUT 200 YEARS.

William Wallace was born in... well this is where the problems begin. We know very little about William Wallace's early life. Historians have suggested he was born somewhere between 1260 and 1278. In fact, we are not even sure where he was born. The best guess we have is Elderslie in Ayrshire.

One place that is often mistaken for Wallace's birthplace is Elderslie in Renfrewshire. If you go there the residents will point to a grassy mound, where a house once stood, and say, "That's where Wallace was born." Strange since it was built at least 200 hundred years after Wallace lived! They will also show you a famous tree and say, "That's Wallace's yew, he used to climb it when he was small." Strange since the tree is not old enough and could not have been planted until hundreds of years after Wallace was dead!

So why is there so much confusion about Wallace's early life? The answer is Blind Harry.

Even though Harry's poem is the oldest surviving record of Wallace's life, we can't trust everything he wrote. It has been proven that Blind Harry simply made stuff up. For example, he describes a battle called the Battle of Biggar, but we know that the battle probably never took place!

PERHAPS WE SHOULD GET OUT OF HERE?

IT'S OK WE DON'T REALLY EXIST.

Blind Harry was born in 1440 and wrote a huge poem about William Wallace's life. The poem was 11,877 stanzas long (that's the posh word for verses) and originally spread over 12 books — no wonder he went blind!

To make matters worse Blind Harry wrote his poem 170 years after Wallace had died. So where did he get all his juicy information? Harry claimed to have used a very old manuscript that was written by Wallace's friend John Blair, but no one has ever been able to find a copy of the book — lucky old Harry!

William Wallace: Fact vs. Fiction

*H*ere are three Wallace facts that some historians would rather you didn't know:

1. He was a noble.

It is pretty clear that William Wallace's father was a very minor noble, not the poor peasant farmer that some films would have you believe.

2. He was big!

Wallace was probably six foot seven inches tall! He was very strong and very good at fighting. His favourite weapon was a huge five foot sword called a claymore. There is a legend that Wallace's sword has survived and is on display at the National Wallace Monument in Stirling.

3. He was Welsh.

In medieval times the surname Wallace was given to someone who had Welsh roots. It seems probable that William Wallace's ancestors originally came from Wales — the country not the animal!

Fighting the English

Even before Edward's armies had attacked Berwick, Wallace had learned to hate the English. In the years immediately prior to John Balliol becoming king, warriors throughout Scotland were fighting against English soldiers. Blind Harry tells us that one of these skirmishes involved Wallace's father and brother, who were killed by an English knight called Fenwick. The pain spurred Wallace into rebellion and in 1291 he struck his first blow against the English.

William Wallace may have been one of the greatest Scottish warriors ever to live, but it seems that his dress sense was about as good as a blind poet.

On a winter's day in 1291, Wallace decided to go for a walk through the streets of Dundee. The giant was dressed in bright green clothes, wearing shoes which were too small and around his waist hung a Scottish dagger called a dirk. He probably looked stupid, but no one dared tell him — would you?

Dundee was ruled by an Englishman called Selby. Unfortunately, Selby's son was a bigheaded bully and, like all bullies, needed a gang to make him feel strong. When Selby's son and his gang saw Wallace they all laughed and stopped him in the street. They told Wallace that he looked as though he had been dressed by the devil, that his jacket was like something a horse would wear and his shoes were too small. However, the bully did like Wallace's dirk and demanded that he give it to him. Our hero refused and the English yob became angry. He then made the biggest mistake of his life and attacked Wallace. The Scotsman grabbed him by his collar, and without thinking, thrust his dirk deep into this heart. His gang could only watch as Wallace let the dead Englishmen drop to the floor.

This left Wallace in a spot of bother. He now had a crowd of angry English soldiers chasing him for bloody revenge, leaving him with no choice but to turn and run for his life. However, before the crowd could reach him, Wallace managed to hide in his uncle's nearby house. The housekeeper, recognising the danger, quickly ordered him to dress in some of her clothes and pretend to be spinning wool. He had only just dressed, when the door burst open and several short-sighted English soldiers rushed into the room. Legend tells us that they failed to recognise Wallace and quickly left. It was too dangerous for Wallace to stay in Dundee, so dressed as a pilgrim he escaped south to Dunipace, but even here he wasn't safe from English soldiers.

One day he went fishing at Irvine Water. He had a good day but as he prepared to leave five English soldiers appeared from nowhere. They demanded that Wallace hand over the fish he had caught. The Brave Scot politely refused and instead generously offered them half his catch, but this

I DON'T MIND THE FISH.
BUT I HOPE HE DOESN'T
THINK I AM CARRYING ALL
OF THOSE HOME FOR HIM.

angered the soldiers and one of them attacked. The unarmed Scotsman dodged the first sword thrust, smacking the man on the cheek with his fishing rod. The soldier fell to the ground, dropping his sword. Wallace picked it up and attacked the soldier on the floor, cutting his neck. The rest of the Englishmen ran at Wallace; the first was slashed on the shoulder and the second had his arm cut clean off, his sword still held firmly in his hand. The remaining men ran away. Legend has it that when they returned to their lord, he just laughed at them.

Death of a Hero

No one knows what happened to Wallace between the years after his escape from Dundee. It seems that he lived as an outlaw, occasionally venturing in disguise into nearby towns. One day, whilst walking through the streets of Ayr, he saw an English soldier bullying a peasant boy. Wallace ordered the Englishmen to leave the boy alone. The soldier became angry and thrust his walking staff at Wallace. Our hero reacted quickly, plunging his dagger into the Englishman's heart. More soldiers soon arrived and Wallace was overpowered. He was taken to a nearby dungeon and left in appalling conditions, with only water and rotten fish to drink and eat. On the day of his trial it was discovered that Wallace had become ill. Thinking the giant Scot was dead, they threw his body onto a nearby dung heap.

When Wallace's friends found the body they noticed he was still breathing, so he was taken into hiding to be nursed back to life. However, word had spread throughout Scotland that Wallace was dead.

In medieval times, people believed lots of strange things. One of these was that prophets could tell the future. One of the most famous prophets was Sir Thomas Rymour.

When he heard that Wallace had not died, he predicted that the Scotsman would lead thousands of men in battle against the English and eventually bring peace to Scotland. People really did believe what Thomas said and when Wallace heard the prediction, he also began to believe it was true.

As soon as Wallace was well enough he left Ayr. Thanks to Thomas Rymour people now believed he was a real leader and started to come from all over Scotland to join him in his fight against the English.

First Blood

A chance soon came for Wallace to show his new power. News arrived that Fenwick, the knight who had killed Wallace's father and brother, was bringing a hoard of stolen gold to Ayr. Wallace decided to ambush the knight and chose to attack at Loudoun Hill, the place his family had been murdered by Fenwick.

armour was made from small rings of steel and was tough enough to resist a blow from a sword. On his head he wore a special helmet called a basinet and in his hands he carried his huge two-handed sword.

Wallace may have been one of the worst dressed men in Scotland, but in battle he took no chances. His armour was typical of the time, with his body, arms and legs covered in a heavy chain mail coat. This type of

Wallace took about 50 men with him into the battle. However, the English had about 180 soldiers, mostly knights mounted on horses. Wallace picked the spot for the battle carefully, choosing a place where the road became so narrow that only two knights could ride next to each other.

The Scottish warriors were dressed differently to Wallace with less armour and carrying huge spears. Wallace told the brave Scots that when the English knights charged, they were to place the butt of the spear into the ground between their feet and hold the point high above their heads.

This was a risky tactic, since it would take a huge amount of courage to stand and wait for a charging horse and knight to run into their spears.

When the knights realised it was an ambush, they didn't fear the Scots and quickly charged, with their sharpened lances held low so they could be driven into the bodies of the unfortunate infantry. However, the Scottish warriors showed real courage and waited, spears in the air, as the knights came closer and closer.

At last the horses smashed into them, and just as Wallace had predicted the sharp spears thrust into the soft bellies of the horses, killing them where they stood. No matter how many times the English ran at the Scots they were stopped by the deadly spears.

During the battle, Wallace fought like a demon, swinging his huge sword about his body, often killing the English soldiers with one mighty blow. Fenwick recognised Wallace as the leader of the Scots and charged his mighty stallion at our hero.

Seeing the knight coming, Wallace dodged his lance and cut at the horse. His sword slashed at the straps which held the saddle in place, causing Fenwick to fall to the ground and before he could get up the Scots were on him, killing him where he lay.

The English were so worried by Wallace and his growing army that they offered a truce lasting 10 months. This was an agreement that no fighting would take place. Wallace agreed. However, the English were still scared and they decided that Wallace should be declared an outlaw, meaning that he could be arrested by anyone who could capture him. Yet this was still not enough to stop the Scotsman. He remained free and continued to build his army.

The Killing of Heselrig

As time passed Wallace became more confident. He moved to Lanark where he could walk around with little harassment. Legend tells us that Wallace fell in love with a girl called Marion. The Sheriff of Lanark was a very important man called Sir William Heselrig and he decided that Wallace needed to be stopped. One day the Scot was confronted in the street by a large group of English soldiers, who forced him to fight. The battle that followed raged through the narrow streets of Lanark. Our hero took refuge in Marion's house and managed to get away to safety through the back door. When Heselrig learned that Wallace had escaped he became very angry. The cruel sheriff marched his men to Marion's house, arrested her and had her put to death.

Wallace and his men were furious and vowed to get revenge. That night they crept back into Lanark and headed straight for Heselrig's house. What happened next is not clear, but Blind Harry tells the best story. Wallace burst into the house, kicking down the large front door with one mighty blow. He then rushed up to the sheriff's room and killed him with a single slice of his sword.

Wallace's attack on Lanark sparked Scotland into rebellion, but William Wallace was not the only rebel leader. In the Highlands was a man called Sir Andrew de Moray. He had also raised a small army to fight against the English. His men were mostly mounted on horses and tended to attack quickly, before disappearing back into the mountains. Soon Scotland became a very dangerous place for the English.

The Battle of Stirling Bridge

Wallace's confidence had now grown to such a level that he felt the time was right for an all-out war against the English. First he attacked and captured Perth, then Dunnottar Castle, followed by Aberdeen where he burned all the English ships in the harbour. Finally, Wallace's army began a long siege of Dundee. It was during this time that Wallace's and Moray's forces finally joined up and by the summer of 1297 had recaptured most of Scotland. King Edward was off in France fighting a war, but their actions didn't go unnoticed by the Earl Warenne, the man left in charge of the English army. He decided he must stop the Scottish rebels. So he gathered together a large English army and headed north in search of Wallace.

This army was made up of three types of soldiers: knights, archers and foot soldiers.

The knights were rich nobles, dressed in the best armour and armed with the best weapons. The archers

Knight

were mostly from Wales and were armed with bows and no armour. The last type was foot soldiers. These were often farmers and would have had the worst weapons and only the simplest armour.

The man in charge of the army was John de Warenne, Earl of Surrey. He had a lot of people telling him what to do, one of whom was Hugh de Cressingham, a very fat and mean priest. He was also the king's tax collector and was hated as much by the English as the Scots!

Unlike the English, the Scottish army didn't have many knights or much cavalry and was made up of normal men, often with poor

Welsh archer

English soldier

Scottish soldier

armour and only carrying a sword, dagger, axe or spear. However, unlike the English, the Scots had something to fight for; they were defending their country and were prepared to fight and die for their freedom. They were led by two men, the mighty William Wallace and his friend, Andrew de Moray.

Map of the Battle of Stirling Bridge

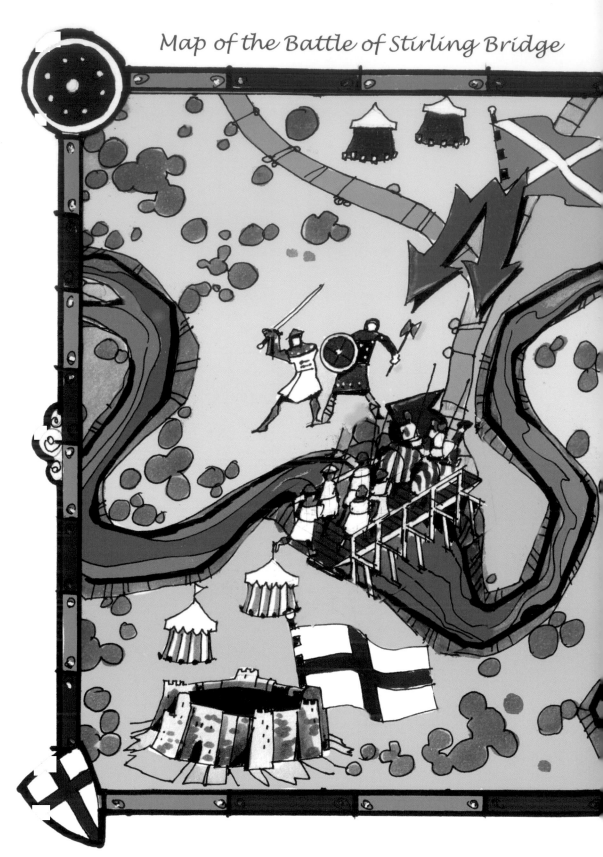

28

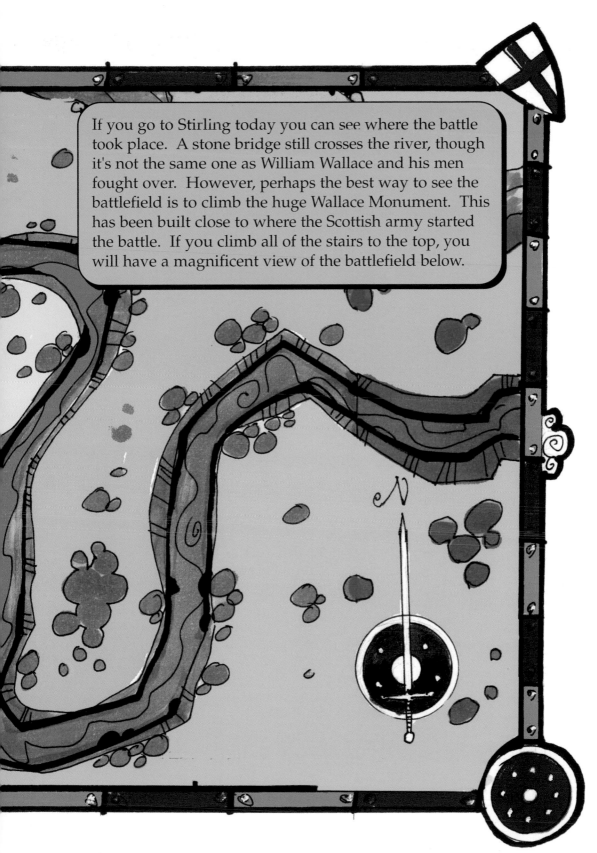

If you go to Stirling today you can see where the battle took place. A stone bridge still crosses the river, though it's not the same one as William Wallace and his men fought over. However, perhaps the best way to see the battlefield is to climb the huge Wallace Monument. This has been built close to where the Scottish army started the battle. If you climb all of the stairs to the top, you will have a magnificent view of the battlefield below.

The two great armies met in the shadow of Stirling Castle. Across the battlefield ran the River Forth, too deep and fast to be crossed anywhere but at a small wooden bridge. The English troops started on the castle side of the river and the Scots on the other. On the Scottish side, the ground was very wet and boggy, making it impossible for the heavy English knights to ride their horses.

On the night before the battle, Warenne gave the order that the English should cross the bridge at first light. Unfortunately, Warenne was an old man and on the morning of the battle he stayed asleep in his bed, long after everyone else

was awake. The result was that 5000 English troops marched over the bridge, stopped, waited and then marched back. The Scots must have been laughing into their porridge!

The English now offered the Scots a chance to give up — which was nice of them! They sent some monks with a message for Wallace. The proud warrior just sent them back telling them that the Scots were here to fight and would be waiting for the English.

It was now about 11 o'clock and after much arguing the English finally gave the order to move over the bridge. It was a slow process and as they

SHHHHHH! YOU WILL WAKE THE OLD MAN UP! YOU KNOW HE NEEDS HIS SLEEP.

crossed, the Scots watched and waited. Leading the English was a brave knight with a strange name— Marmaduke Tweng.

Wallace watched from a hill, high above the battlefield, called Abbey Craig. The place he stood is today marked by a huge building called the Wallace Monument. He knew that his attack must be timed perfectly. If he waited too long, the number of English soldiers crossing would be too great and the Scots would be unable to beat them. If he didn't wait long enough, too few English soldiers would cross the river and most of the English would survive. At last Wallace felt the time was right. He lifted a great horn to his lips and, with a single blow, signalled the Scottish to attack.

The Scots rushed forward with a terrifying war cry. Before the battle, a section of the men had been carefully chosen and ordered to capture the bridge. These men bravely rushed into the English lines, quickly fighting through and forcing their way onto the bridge. This meant that the English couldn't bring any more troops over the river. It also meant that the English soldiers on the Scottish side of the river were trapped with no escape. The remaining Scottish army now smashed into the English lines. The marshy ground made it impossible for the heavy English knights to charge and the battle turned into hundreds of small and bloody fights. As it raged on, the English began to realise that they were surrounded and panic spread through the ranks.

There were now more Scottish warriors fighting than English soldiers and it was clear that the Scots were winning. As things became increasingly desperate for the English, many of their knights tried to get away by riding straight into the river.

However, since they were still dressed in their full armour most were dragged away and drowned by the current. One English knight didn't panic—he was brave Marmaduke Tweng. He had fought in many battles, and knew his only chance of survival was not to panic and somehow get across the river. So he calmly gathered together his men and charged headlong towards the bridge. Even though the Scottish soldiers were all around him, he still managed to fight his way through, skilfully cutting a path with his sword. Once he was onto the wooden bridge he swung his sword with such might that the Scottish were unable to stop him getting back over the river to safety.

GET A MOVE ON!

Tweng was one of the few English knights to survive the battle. The medieval bridge was not designed to have hundreds of men and knights fighting for their lives on it. Soon it began to creak and buckle and within minutes it had collapsed into the river. Now the English on the safe side of the river could do nothing but watch as the Scottish warriors continued their attack. The Scots sensed victory was near and continued to fight without mercy. Across the battlefield the Scottish warriors could be heard screaming, "On them! On them!" as the slaughter of the English began.

Old man Warenne knew his men were defeated and like all beaten bullies he turned and ran. Well he didn't actually run; it was his horse that did the running, he just did the sitting, but you know what I mean. In fact, he ran so hard that he didn't stop until he got to Berwick. One story tells us that when he finally got off his poor horse, the animal just keeled over and dropped down dead from exhaustion!

Warenne was lucky to escape; one man who was not so lucky was the fat priest, Cressingham. He had been one of the first men to cross the bridge and some accounts do survive of what happened to him. It is thought that when Cressingham realised the battle was lost, he decided to get back across the river. The problem was that since he was so fat, as he tried to turn his horse around, he slipped, lost his balance and fell off! His huge body became stuck in the mud and he died under a combination of horses' hooves and Scottish blades. After the battle, when the Scots found the body of the hated tax collector, they decided to make an example of him. What they did was pretty horrible, so if you are a bit squeamish I suggest you look away now …

First they took off his armour…

Then they removed his clothes…

Finally they took off his skin!!

Yes, they skinned poor Cressingham.

Many legends exist as to what happened to the skin, some say Wallace used it to make a grip for his sword, others say he made a saddle for his horse. We will never know what actually happened, but the most likely story is that the hide was cut into small pieces and carried away by all the men Cressingham had been mean to whilst alive.

The Battle of Stirling Bridge was over and Wallace was finally the true leader of Scotland. However, when King Edward found out what happened he was extremely angry — he was so angry he probably turned purple. He decided that the only way to get rid of the upstart Wallace was to do it himself.

Taking the Fight to the English

Straight after the Battle of Stirling Bridge, Wallace set up his headquarters at Stirling Castle. Everyone knew that it wouldn't be long before the angry King Edward was in Scotland looking for revenge. However the Scots had won their freedom and they weren't about to give it up without a fight.

Even though the Battle of Stirling Bridge had been a great success for the Scots, it was not all good. During the battle Andrew de Moray had been injured and a few weeks later he died from his wounds. This left Wallace as the undisputed leader of Scotland, but he made it clear that the true leader was still King John.

Do you remember him? King of Scotland … Toom Tabard … humiliated by Edward … ran away to France? Well I am not surprised if you had forgotten all about him.

In fact, lots of Scots had forgotten all about John, especially since he was off hiding across the Channel.

Now Wallace was ready to take the war to England. He rounded up his men and headed south looking for … well … money! It was Wallace's plan to invade England and steal as much as he could carry. He didn't really want to fight another big battle, he just wanted to teach King Edward a lesson. So on 18th October 1297, Wallace's army crossed the river Tweed into England.

With no English army to stop the Scots they set about looting the whole of Cumbria. Wallace made his headquarters in the Forest of Rothbury and sent out his men to attack all the nearby towns and villages. When they finally got bored and there was nothing left to steal, the army decided to head south to County Durham. It was winter when they set out and the weather was already pretty bad, but on the

8th November a terrible storm began to blow. It was so bad that the Scots decided to turn around and return to their nice warm homes. Some people say the storm was God telling the Scots to go home — but of course these people are English!

When Wallace finally got back to Scotland the people wanted to show him how much they liked him and on Christmas 1297, he was made a knight. From that day on he was to be known as Sir William Wallace. This still left the small problem of who was going to rule Scotland. The true king was John Balliol, but he had given up the crown after the Battle of Dunbar. This meant that the only real leader was Wallace, so at the end of 1297 he was made Guardian of Scotland.

RIGHT LADS IT'S RAINING, LET'S GO HOME.

I THINK IT WOULD BE BEST IF WE WENT HOME. WE DON'T WANT TO MAKE HIM ANGRY! YOU KNOW WHAT HE GETS LIKE WHEN HE'S ANGRY.

In January 1298 the English held a meeting at York. It was decided that an army should be formed in Newcastle. Old man Warenne, the general beaten at the Battle of Stirling Bridge, was once again put in charge and he quickly headed north. It was all going well until he reached Kelso. Here he stopped and refused to go any further! Legend says that Wallace had formed a small band of cavalry and was harassing Earl Warenne's men. This scared the earl. This isn't really that much of a surprise, since Wallace and his men had already beaten the Englishman in the Battle of Stirling Bridge.

On 14th March 1298, everything changed when King Edward finally returned from France. He was still very, very angry and as soon as his feet hit English soil he headed north to Scotland. At last Edward and Wallace would meet face-to-face in battle and the winner would rule Scotland — well almost!

The Battle of Falkirk

Wallace was ready for Edward. Since the Battle of Stirling Bridge, he had been busy organising his army. It was done in the same way as the ancient Romans, with Centurions looking after groups of 100 men. He made sure that the best fighters and leaders were put in charge of commanding his army in battle. Wallace also introduced a new way of fighting – called a schiltrom. The men were organised into small groups and armed with very long spears. They then arranged themselves so the spears stuck out in all directions – a bit like a hedgehog. The warriors at the front would kneel on the floor and the men behind would push their spears over the front rank's shoulders. The men practised and practised forming into the schiltrom until they could do it perfectly.

Unlike Warenne, King Edward was an experienced solider and he meant business. As soon as he arrived in England he set about preparing for war.

The problem for the king was that Wallace didn't want to fight. This wasn't because the Brave Scot was a coward, but because he had a plan to beat the English. Wallace intended to starve them! Before the king's army had arrived, Wallace's men had destroyed all the food, crops and even some towns and villages in the advancing army's path.

King Edward and his army headed north and Wallace's plan

40

soon began to work. The English were starving and with no food the king was soon ready to turn around and head home. Then his luck changed. A message came to him that the Scottish army was camped just a few miles away. Without wasting any time the English saddled up and marched after the Scots. They only stopped to sleep, lying down next to their horses. In the dark something scared the king's horse and it kicked out, hitting Edward and breaking his ribs. However, he was not able to let on to his men and next morning he bravely mounted his horse and carried on as if nothing was wrong.

The English army continued to march until it caught sight of the Scots and then, knowing battle was close, stopped so the priests could say Mass. When they emerged from their prayers, it was clear that the Scottish army had formed up, on the slope of a hill, a few miles from their position. The Battle of Falkirk was about to begin!

However, this leaves one really BIG question. Why did Wallace stop and fight? His tactics were working, the English were tired and hungry and many of their soldiers wanted to go home. So, why risk it all in one battle? The answer is probably that Wallace had no choice. The king's march

from Edinburgh had caught him by surprise and once the two armies were close enough, the only option was to fight.

The Scottish knew the biggest threat they faced was from the English knights. So they deployed in a way that would stop the horsemen as much as possible. Firstly, the Scots were on the slope of a hill. This meant that anyone charging up the hill would quickly become very tired. Secondly, they had formed into the schiltrom formation with spears sticking out in all directions. Therefore, any horses running into the schiltrom would be skewered and killed. Finally, Wallace's army was also helped by the ground between the English and Scots. It was very marshy and no English knights would be able to charge straight over it and up the hill.

The English formed up into four groups on the opposite side of the valley. There were three groups of cavalry and one large group of infantry. This group was not only made up of both English and Welsh troops, but also special archers called longbow men. These fired a new type of bow called a longbow. It was about 6 feet long and launched an arrow much further than a normal bow and with so much power that the arrow could even pierce armour!

Edward was eager to get the battle started and he ordered his Welsh soldiers to attack first. Now, the Welshmen didn't like Edward, after all he had invaded their country. In fact, they didn't trust him as far as they could throw him and when the order to advance was given, they thought the king was sending them to their death and they refused to attack.

Edward was furious and instead ordered the first wave of knights forward. They were commanded by three earls — the Earl of Norfolk, the Earl of Hereford and the Earl of Lincoln. The horses thundered towards the Scots, their armour and swords flashing in the sunlight, gaining more and more speed. Then, just as they were about to start up the slope to flatten the Scots they ... well ... stopped ... stuck in the mud. Unknown to the English, the ground in front of the Scots was very, very wet and when the heavy horses rode into it, they just sank. Maybe the English were using some new comedy tactics? The three earls had no choice but to retreat out of the marsh and charge off to the right.

Edward was now even angrier — I suspect he may even have turned that funny shade of purple again. In a rage he ordered his second wave of knights into the attack. They were commanded by Bishop

Bek, who seemed to be cleverer that the three earls. He started off at a much slower pace and instead of running into the marsh he ordered his horsemen to ride to the left and avoid any more sinking horses. Once Bek was across a small stream that ran through the battlefield, he stopped and waited for King Edward. However, Edward was cautious and advanced slowly with the third group of cavalry. The English knights were pretty keen to get into battle and soon got

I KNEW WE WOULD BE BETTER OFF ON THE SCOTTISH SIDE.

tired of waiting for their king. As they started to attack, Bishop Bek ordered them to stop, but their reply was rather rude. It went something like, "Go and sing a hymn and let us knights do the fighting" — charming!

So finally the English knights began to attack the Scottish schiltroms; on the left Bek's men smashed into the Scots and on the right the three earls' men did their best to cause havoc. The horses and their riders threw themselves at the schiltroms and the lethal spiky spears. But guess what…as tonnes of horse flesh and armoured knights smashed in the Scottish warriors, do you know what happened?

Nothing!
Well not nothing. In fact hundreds

of horses and English knights were pierced by the spears and died horrible and painful deaths, but the Scots stayed put. The knights had failed to break into the formation and they had no choice but to turn around and head back down the slope.

Wallace's men had survived the knights' first attack, but they had not got away scot-free. Wallace had only a small amount of cavalry and they had been placed behind the schiltroms to protect them from enemy archers. However, when they saw the mighty English knights fall upon the Scottish infantry, they turned around and ran away. Simple as that, they up and left! This was a real blow to the Scottish. You see, though schiltroms could withstand a few hundred fully armoured English knights, one thing that did scare them was…ghosts…no sorry I was joking, what scared them was… arrows! When the schiltrom was formed it couldn't move. This meant that if enemy bowmen got close enough to fire an arrow, the infantry could do nothing but stand and wait to die. Now Wallace wasn't stupid, he knew this. Though he had only a few cavalry, they were doing a very important job. He had positioned them behind the schiltroms and told them to attack any English bowmen who got too close, but with the Scottish cavalry now half way back to Stirling, the English archers were free to advance and fire at will.

Edward, seeing the Scottish cavalry had gone, once again ordered his knights to attack. This time they ignored the schiltroms and instead thundered down onto the vulnerable Scottish archers. Finally, the English king turned to his bowman and sent them into the battle. Soon the mighty longbows were in range and the sky was blackened with a cloud of deadly arrows, which fell like rain. The brave Scots had no chance. Hundreds died, unable to escape the slaughter.

Finally Edward sensed his time had come and he once again sent his knights into the battle. This time the schiltroms were weak and as the huge mass of horses ran up the hill, the Scottish warriors knew the end was near and with no choice, many just turned and ran. Without mercy the English horses smashed into the men. The battle and the Scottish dream of freedom was over and King Edward was victorious.

Map of the Battle of Falkirk

Wallace in Exile

William Wallace managed to escape from the Battle of Falkirk alive. However, with his army beaten and the English troops controlling the Lowlands of Scotland, his power was gone. Soon after the battle he gave up being Guardian of Scotland and went into hiding.

As for King Edward, things weren't much better. He had beaten Wallace, but the cost was high. His men were starving and he had no choice but to head back to England. First he marched south to Ayr, then to Dumfries and finally reached Carlisle and English soil on the 8th September 1298.

The march had been horrendous, with more and more men dying of starvation and disease as each day passed. In fact, more men died after the battle than were killed by Scottish swords. When they reached safety, almost all of the English horses were dead, with many of them being eaten by the hungry soldiers.

So what happened to Wallace? Well, we don't really know. We do know that on 24th August he attacked an English convoy carrying supplies just outside Edinburgh. We also know that shortly after this he set sail for France.

HAS ANYONE SEEN MY HORSE?

However, what we don't know is what happened to him over the next few years. The only person that tells us anything about what happened is Blind Harry and we all know how unreliable he can be! Anyway, this is what Blind Harry tells us: Soon after setting sail for France, William Wallace's ship was attacked by Thomas de Longueville and his band of pirates. Harry explains how the pirate ship drew alongside Wallace's boat and the pirate leader jumped on board. He must have had the shock of his life when he realised he was trying to rob the famous Scottish knight, Sir William Wallace. Anyway, Wallace acted as all good heroes should and managed to capture the pirate without killing him. Thomas was so grateful that his life had been spared that he promised to give up pirating forever and become a good boy.

Betrayed

By July 1304 most of Scotland was in English hands. King Edward's persistent attacks had slowly won back most of the Lowlands. To make matters worse, most of the Scottish knights had surrendered to Edward. However, one man refused to give in to English rule — Sir William Wallace. As we have already worked out, King Edward was a pretty angry man, so as you might imagine Wallace's refusal to surrender did nothing to help his mood. Edward was very keen to catch our Brave Scot and he offered a large reward for his capture. In the meantime, Wallace had returned to Scotland and roamed the countryside, hiding from the English and taking refuge with friends. Slowly things became more and more desperate for Wallace, but by 1305 he was still free.

The man who finally captured Wallace was Sir John de Menteith. He was a Scottish knight who came from a very important family. He had fought for the Scots at the Battle of Dunbar but had been captured. However, he soon changed sides and fought for Edward in France.

In 1298 he returned to Scotland and once again swapped sides to fight for the Scottish, but again, in 1303, he joined the English. In fact, it seems that Menteith couldn't really make his mind up exactly who he was fighting for!

The thing is that Menteith wasn't the only Scottish knight that King Edward had ordered to find Wallace. It's just that these other knights, including the future king of Scotland, Robert Bruce, only pretended to be looking for our hero.

Menteith knew that King Edward was very powerful and if he refused, the king would take his lands and probably have him killed. So Menteith had no choice but to try and capture Wallace. The problem for Wallace was that he tried too hard!

The knight soon learned that Wallace was hiding in a nearby

farmhouse. Menteith bribed one of Wallace's servants and told him to take the Scot's mighty sword when he was sleeping. So, in the middle of the night, Menteith's men surrounded the house. When the servant came out with the sword, Menteith ordered his men in. The attackers burst into Wallace's room, waking the huge Scot. Without hesitation, he dived for his sword, only to find it was gone. But even with only his bare hands, Wallace managed to kill a number of the men before he was finally captured.

Our Brave Scot was tied firmly to a horse and taken south to Carlisle. The group travelled at night and kept away from towns and villages. Once in Carlisle he was thrown in the castle's dungeon overnight before being tied once again to a horse for the march south.

The journey took 17 days and news of the Scottish rebel's capture spread quickly. As he got closer and closer to London, more and more people came into the streets to see the famous outlaw. When he finally reached the capital, the crowds were so large that Wallace and his captors had to stop and take refuge in a nearby house. King Edward had arranged for a huge trial to take place at Westminster Hall and the next morning Wallace was led on horseback to the building. The crowds followed him everywhere, jeering, shouting and throwing things at him.

Westminster Hall is still there today and is part of the Houses of Parliament. It is a huge room and it was here that the court sat, ready for Wallace. The Scot was led in and a crown of leaves placed on his head. No one knows why this was done; some say it was tradition, others say it was because he had once said he would be king. The trial then began. You must remember that this was in medieval times. It was not like today when both sides have lawyers, witnesses, evidence and an impartial judge. This was King Edward's chance to humiliate his enemy. Wallace was given no opportunity to defend himself or his actions. In fact, as English law stood, since Wallace had already been declared an outlaw the king could just have killed him on the spot — but Edward wanted more than that: he wanted revenge.

Slowly a list of charges was read out. The most important of these was treason, which means you have betrayed your king or country. The problem was that Wallace had never accepted that England was his country or King Edward his king. The Scot had always insisted that he was fighting for King John NOT King Edward! He was also charged with murdering William de Heselrig, Sheriff of Lanark, and trying to make people fight against King Edward, which he did in two battles. There was a long list of other things which Wallace was said to have done.

Some were true, some were false and many were just downright lies. However, it made no difference since Wallace was never given a chance to argue against any of the charges. The only thing Wallace said during the whole trial was that he was not a traitor, since Edward was not his king. Yet, even as Wallace realised his fate was sealed, he stood proud, his chest thrust forward and his head held high. A Brave Scot to the end.

Hanged, Drawn and Quartered

At last it was all over and King Edward decided the sentence. The exact words that were spoken at the trial have been written down and have survived until today — here are some of them:

It was decided that Wallace should be
'hanged, and afterwards taken down from the gallows.'

Then while alive, his
'heart, the liver and lungs as well as all the other intestines…cast into the fire and burnt.'

Finally Wallace's body was
'to be cut up and divided into four parts, and that one quarter be hung on a gibbet at Newcastle-upon-Tyne, another quarter at Berwick, a third quarter at Stirling, and the fourth at St Johnston, as a warning and a deterrent to all that pass by and behold them.'

Horrible King Edward's Revenge

Wallace was dragged from Westminster Hall, stripped naked and tied to a wooden cart. He was put on his back with his head near the floor. It was only four miles to the place of execution but the journey would have taken hours. As the helpless Wallace was taken through the crowds, people pushed forwards and punched and kicked his body. Some threw rubbish, some rotting meat and some even threw poo.

The cart came to a halt at what is today King Street in Smithfield.

Wallace would have been nearly unconscious and bleeding from cuts all over his naked body. He was untied from the cart and taken to the foot of the gallows. Here he was made to climb the tall ladder and once at the top a rope was placed around his neck and he was pushed off. The crowd cheered as Wallace's body swung from the rope. However, the executioner had to make sure he did not die. So he waited until our hero was gasping for his last breath and then cut him down.

Now the Brave Scot was barely alive but he was picked up and placed on the stage in front of the jeering crowd.

WARNING!

I must warn you that what happens next is pretty horrible … but it's history; it's the truth and it's what happened to our brave warrior … so here goes. Whilst he was still alive, the executioner cut open Wallace's stomach and took out his intestines. These were pushed in front of Wallace's face so he could see them clearly and then they were thrown onto a fire. At this point the crowd cheered even more loudly and became even more excited. Next the executioner pushed his hand deep into Wallace's chest and pulled out his heart. It was thrust high above his head, still beating, for the crowd to enjoy. Mercifully Wallace would now have been dead but the punishment was not over. After his heart had been removed, next came his liver and finally his lungs.

Now you might think that this would be enough but Edward hadn't finished. Wallace's body was laid on the floor and, using an axe, the executioner cut his head off with one blow. Even now it was still not over. What was left of the body was cut into four parts — two arms and two legs. These were then taken and displayed for all to see. The head was dipped in tar to stop it decaying and placed on a spear on London bridge. The right arm was hung in Newcastle–upon–Tyne, the left arm in Stirling, the right leg in Berwick and the left leg in Perth.

Finally Wallace was dead and King Edward had his way. Scotland was in English hands and all of the Scottish

rebels had been killed or bribed or put in prison.
So had Wallace died in vain?
Had his rebellion been for nothing?

Well — NO!

Wallace had achieved one very important thing — he had taught the Scottish nation that if they came together as one people, as Scottish people, they could defeat even the biggest and strongest enemy. Though Edward thought Scotland was at last in his control, the peace wouldn't last long. Within years, a Scottish king, a fellow Brave Scot called Robert Bruce, would rise once again against English rule and the two great nations would be at war — but that's another story.